The History of Harborne Hall

by
Frances Wilmot

Meridian Books
(in association with the Multi-Faith Centre)

Published 1991 by Meridian Books (in association with the Multi-Faith Centre, Birmingham)
© The Multi-Faith Centre, Birmingham 1991

British Library Cataloguing-in-Publication Data
A catalogue record for this book is available from the British Library

ISBN 1 869922 17 4

Meridian Books
40 Hadzor Road
Oldbury
Warley
West Midlands
B68 9LA

Printed by Aston University

Contents

Preface...iv

Introduction...v

Acknowledgements...v

Chapter 1   Early History of Harborne: 1086-1499........................ 1

Chapter 2   The Manor of Harborne: 1500-1786 2

Chapter 3   Harborne Hall in the Georgian Era: 1786-1836 5

Chapter 4   Harborne Hall in Victorian Times: 1837-1883 11

Chapter 5   Extensions to Harborne Hall: 1884-1901.................... 26

Chapter 6   Edwardian Times: 1902-1909 33

Chapter 7   First World War: 1914-1918 36

Chapter 8   Harborne Hall in the Twentieth Century: 1919-1991 .. 39

Bibliography.. 47

Index.. 48

Preface

In 1988, thanks to the generosity of the Sisters of La Retraite, Harborne Hall became the location for the work of the Multi-Faith Centre — a Foundation for Education and Citizenship, established in Birmingham in 1981.

During the academic year 1990/91, 7362 clients availed themselves of the excellent residential and non-residential Conference facilities of the Hall. "What is the history of this place?" became a very familiar question as groups — many of them from Europe — admired the long stained glass windows, wood panelling and ornate wrought ironwork of the staircase.

It so happened that at the conclusion of one of the day programmes I met Paul Wilmot, an executive of the Children's Society, who mentioned that his ancestors had lived in the Hall over a period. When I told him that we had begun a research project on its history I discovered that his wife, a librarian, had portraits and documentation related to his family. We arranged to meet and, as a result, the Research Project was born. Nine months later it was completed, thanks in large measure to the commitment and zeal of Frances Wilmot, wife of the great great grandson of Edward Wilmot.

The publication of the book is timed to coincide with the opening of a mounted exhibition in December 1991 on the history of Harborne Hall and its occupants throughout the centuries.

Dr Mary Hall
Executive Director
Harborne Hall Multi-Faith Centre
Old Church Road
Harborne
Birmingham B17 0BD

Introduction

Harborne Hall has 200 years of history going back to the end of the eighteenth century, being part of the Manor of Harborne and Smethwick which dates back to the Norman Conquest.

Built by a wealthy nailmaster who was Lord of the Manor of Harborne, the Hall was occupied for many years by the Simcox family. In Victorian times the occupants of the Hall included a jeweller, an artist, two ecclesiastical metal manufacturers and members of the well-known Chamberlain and Nettlefold families of Birmingham.

With its history linked with industrial Birmingham the Hall subsequently became a home for refugees before being transformed into a hospital for wounded soldiers in the First World War. It later became a boys' school, a convent and finally the Multi-Faith Centre which commemorated its tenth anniversary in 1991 — in the same year that Harborne celebrated its centenary connection with the city of Birmingham.

The book has been carefully researched and includes original material from families and other persons connected with the Hall. I would like to thank everyone who sent in personal contributions or helped my research — and especially Leslie Blennerhassett for all his photographic work.

Frances Wilmot

Acknowledgements

The help given by the following persons and organisations is gratefully acknowledged.

Avery Historical Museum, GEC Avery Ltd., Smethwick
Barton, R
Birmingham Library Services
Blennerhassett, Leslie E
Brown, John
Dean, Sister Mary
GKN plc, Redditch
Hall, Mary
Harborne Public Library
Hefford, Elizabeth
Jackson, Albert E.
Jones, Jill
La Retraite Archives, London
Partridge, Diana C.
Royal Warwickshire Regimental Museum, St John's, Warwick
Sheridan, Sister Ellen
Smethwick Public Library
Southworth, Rosemary
Terry, G.V.
The Rt. Revd. Mark Santer, Bishop of Birmingham
Walmsley, Cyril R.
Wild, Glenys (Birmingham Museums and Art Gallery)
and my husband Paul for his help and encouragement in writing this book.

Harborne Hall, painted in 1867 by Mary Jane Roberts

Chapter 1

Early History of Harborne: 1086-1499

The name Harborne means "boundary brook" — Harborne is bounded by the Bourne and Chad Brooks.

The Domesday Book of 1086 has the earliest known reference to Harborne, known as "Horeborne", being a manor in the Bunter lands of West Birmingham in the Staffordshire Uplands. These lands had an average population of three recorded adults per square mile. Harborne was valued at £1. The Domesday entry for Harborne was as follows:

"In Harborne there was land for 1 plough, held by Robert; in Smethwick there was land for 2 ploughs and in Tipton, 5 ploughs, held by William. In these two hamlets were 7 ploughs and 60 villeins and 22 borderers with 25 ploughs. Amongst them all were 52 acres of meadow and a mill."

The Bishop of Chester held Harborne, Smethwick and Tipton as a feudal baron under William the Conqueror. It was part of the great manor of Longdon, near Lichfield, an area comprising thirty manors, townships and villages. Harborne was probably a tiny hamlet near a spring. (Overlordship of the Manor of Harborne and Smethwick continued in the hands of the Bishops of Coventry and Lichfield until 1538, when it was surrendered to Henry VIII.)

In 1160 in the time of Henry II, the 'Lord of Horeborne' was Ralph, the 'sewer' or steward to Walter Durdent, Bishop of Lichfield. In 1166 Henry FitzGerald, Chamberlain to the Queen of Henry II, held Harborne and Smethwick from the Bishop of Coventry — two manors within a single parish.

In 1217 Harborne church is mentioned for the first time in the will of Warin FitzGerald, Lord of the Manor of Harborne and Chamberlain to King John and King Henry III. He left to his daughter, Margaret de Redvers, the 'advowson' or right to appoint the church priest in Harborne — she had held Harborne and Smethwick as part of her marriage portion. She granted the manor to Halesowen Abbey which retained it until 1538.

In 1255 the Bishop of Chester held the manor of Longdon from Henry III in baronry — 'Horeborn' manor consisted of 300 acres. Two men were named as the vicars of Harborne, Robert de Radinges and Henry de Wingham.

In 1327 a Lay Subsidy Roll granted by the first parliament of Edward III shows the population of Harborne to be only nine persons considered rich enough "to contribute towards the defence of the realm aginst the Scotch". All earls, barons, knights, citizens and burgesses had to pay the tax of one twentieth of the value of their movable goods, Harborne contributing the sum total of £1. 0. 6d.

Henry VI's Patent Rolls of 1429-1436 listed two men in Harborne appointed as Guardians of the Peace, gentry selected by knights of the shire who were required to take an oath against "assisting peace-breakers". The two men were John Whatecroft, Esquire and Nicolas Thyknes, gentleman.

Chapter 2

The Manor of Harborne: 1500-1786

In the reign of Henry VIII, in 1538, Harborne church began its first parish registers of births, marriages and deaths. In this year Halesowen Abbey surrendered the manor of Harborne to the King at the dissolution of the monasteries. The overlordship of the manor was granted in 1546 to Sir William Paget as pertaining to the manor of Longdon, Staffordshire. He held the manorial rights but the Abbey lands, tithes and advowson went to the Dudley family.

Sir William Paget (1505-1563) was granted many lands including that of Beaudesert in Staffordshire, which became the chief seat of his family. He was knighted in 1537 by Henry VIII and when the marriage of Anne of Cleves was arranged he was appointed her secretary. In 1540 he became clerk to the privy council and was granted Arms the following year. In 1543 he was appointed as one of the Secretaries of State which brought him into very close relations with Henry VIII, involving him in many political matters. The king bequeathed him some money in his will and appointed him as one of the governors of young Prince Edward during his minority. He became comptroller of King Edward VI's household and was appointed one of the lords lieutenant for Staffordshire and Middlesex in 1551. In 1552 he was found to have made large profits for himself at the expense of the crown and all his estates were placed at the king's disposal, until he paid his debts the following year. After the death of Edward VI he took a prominent part in the coronation of Queen Mary and became a member of her privy council, becoming Lord Privy Seal until Queen Elizabeth's accession. He died in 1563, in Middlesex — a monument was erected to his memory in Lichfield Cathedral and there was a portrait painted of him by the artist Holbein.

The manor of Harborne and Smethwick was granted with Halesowen in 1538 to Sir John Dudley, Duke of Northumberland, who was found guilty of treason and beheaded in 1553 for trying to settle the crown on the Protestant Lady Jane Grey, after the death of Henry VIII. Dudley was the son of Edmund Dudley, Henry VIII's chief administrator, who had been beheaded at the beginning of the king's reign. Sir John Dudley was one of the ablest men of his time after the death of Henry VIII. He was an experienced soldier, keen politician and skilful administrator; in the course of twenty years he had become Lord High Admiral, Viscount Lisle, Earl of Warwick and High Chamberlain of England. He also pillaged unscrupulously from religious houses and the church. A first class athlete, (the finest jouster of his day), he was an elegant, handsome and accomplished courtier and had been one of Henry VIII's most valued servants. After Henry's death he plotted to transfer the succession of the crown to his family — namely Lady Jane Grey, wife of his son Guildford in a political marriage. He persuaded the dying young King Edward VI to sign a document disinheriting Mary and Elizabeth Tudor in favour of Jane, his cousin, whose claim was through her being great granddaughter of Henry VII.

When Edward VI died on 6th July 1553 Dudley caused the Lady Jane Grey to be proclaimed Queen, taking arms against the Catholic Princess Mary, the rightful queen. His forces deserted him and he was arrested, taken to the Tower and beheaded for high treason on 22nd July. Although he had been recently supporting the Protestant Jane, he avowed himself Catholic at the scaffold and was executed after Mary had been proclaimed Queen. The hapless sixteen year old Jane was imprisoned and executed in 1554. After his death his estates were forfeited to the crown but were reinstated in 1554 by Queen Mary to his nephew Edward, Lord Dudley. In 1618 the family sold them to the Cornwallis family in the reign of James I.

Sir Charles Cornwallis and his brother Sir Thomas bought the manor of Harborne and Smethwick, which included 400 acres of land, 40 acres of meadow, 300 acres of pasture and 60 acres of wood for the sum of £400. Sir Charles was a courtier and diplomat and became the first known residing Lord of the Manor in Harborne. He had been a Member of Parliament for Norfolk since 1604, was sent to Spain as resident ambassador and became, in 1610, the treasurer of the household of Henry, Prince of Wales, until the Prince's sudden death in 1612. In 1613 he had been sent to Ireland to investigate Irish grievances and was arrested a year later for suspected treason against James I, being imprisoned in the Tower for a year. He retired to Harborne late in life, where he died in 1629 and was buried at St Giles in the Field, London. After Sir Charles's death his grandson Charles (of Blakeley Hall, Halesowen) held the manor in 1634, selling it in 1661 to Thomas Foley of Witley Court and Henry Glover of Stourbridge, for the sum of £660.

Thomas Foley (1617-1677) was the eldest son of Richard Foley who was an iron manufacturer in Stourbridge. His father had discovered a process of 'splitting' (by secretly visiting Swedish ironworks disguised as a fiddler) which had enabled him to erect machines for the process. Thomas amassed a large fortune from the iron industry, increased by a wealthy marriage. He acquired much extensive property, settling at Witley Court in later life. He secured valuable church patronage at Kidderminster and was described by a contemporary as "a truly honest man", being a Member of Parliament for Bewdley in 1660 and High Sheriff of Worcestershire. In 1667 he founded Old Swinford Hospital for sixty poor boys, a school which still exists near Stourbridge. It originally fed, clothed and educated selected boys from different parishes in Worcestershire and Staffordshire, free of charge. The boys were apprenticed afterwards to trades, financed by the school. Harborne originally had the privilege of sending five boys to this school and was a charity much valued by the poor. The school has a portrait of Thomas Foley, who died and was buried at Witley in 1677.

In 1666 the Hearth Tax, or chimney tax, payable to Charles II, was charged to ninety-one inhabitants of Harborne, sixty being exempt. Two shillings had to be paid by all tax-payers which was an extremely profitable source of income for the King, until it ceased in 1689.

In 1710, in the reign of Queen Anne, the manor of Harborne and

3

Smethwick changed hands again, the Foley family disposing of their possession to George Birch and Henry Hinckley. The manor was split, with Smethwick going to the Hinckley family and Harborne to George Birch. The Birch family were landowners and residents of Harborne for many generations and lived at a mansion called Holt Hill (now demolished) which was near the site of Great Arthur Street, Smethwick. The Birch's ancestry goes back to Thomas Birch, a 'nailer' of Erdington in Elizabethan times. A Birch pedigree in Burke's *Landed Gentry* states that George Birch's father, George, was a tenant of Harborne Hall in the seventeenth century but it must have been an earlier building as Harborne Hall appears to have been built after 1786.

It is likely there was a traditional manor house in Harborne, the seat of the Lord of the Manor, which was known as "the Hall", from Elizabethan times. The Birch family may have been tenants of Charles Cornwallis of Blakeley Hall between 1634 and 1661, occupying "the Hall". They were similarly tenants of the Foley family until 1710 when George Birch purchased the Manor and lands, becoming the residing Lord of the Manor. The Lord of the Manor of Harborne was a very important position. Harborne had been regarded as an important village from Elizabethan times, being marked in 1576 on Saxton's map.

George Birch's son Sir Thomas was Lord of the Manor of Harborne in 1730 and a Justice of Common Pleas. His son George Birch sold the manor of Harborne to Thomas Green in the reign of George III, after 1786, having inherited the more lucrative manor of Hamstead.

It seems that Thomas Green was the person who built Harborne Hall but due to lack of documentary evidence nothing is proven. The style of the earliest part of the Hall would suggest late eighteenth century but many parts of it were rebuilt in the nineteenth century.

Chapter 3

Harborne Hall in the Georgian Era: 1786-1836

Thomas Green 1731-1803

Thomas Green, Lord of the Manor of Harborne, was probably the first owner and builder of Harborne Hall. He was a nailmaster who made a considerable fortune in the iron trade which enabled him to purchase the Manor of Harborne from George Birch, some time after 1786, and some land in Harborne.

He owned a warehouse at the top of Fellowes Lane, Harborne, and probably purchased some land from the Piner family to build Harborne House, now called Bishop's Croft. He also built Harborne Hall on this land for his daughter Elizabeth, who was the wife of George Simcox.

Presterne recalls in his book *Harborne Once Upon A Time* that the building of Harborne Hall caused a few problems. Bricks were carried in panniers on the backs of twenty seven donkeys from Lappal Tunnel, three miles distant. The roads at that time were impassable before the days of Macadam. The donkey owner was "a gypsy-like man with a bludgeon in his hand", being the one and only haulier in the parish.

The Hall was probably built on the site of an earlier mediaeval or Elizabethan building — architectural plans or archaeological excavations would ascertain without any doubt the evidence of this building. Thomas Green rebuilt the Hall in the Georgian period, probably as depicted in a painting by Mary Jane Roberts, an occupant of Harborne Hall in 1867. Evidence from architectural plans made in 1884 suggest it was L-shaped with a large Tuscan porch on the main entrance. There is also a sketch by an artistic member of the Simcox family, made in the early nineteenth century, which shows the Hall with a two storey Regency bow at the east end. This sketch is included in a book entitled *Views Of Harborne, Staffordshire* which is held by the Lord Bishop of Birmingham in Bishop's Croft.

Thomas Green was known as "Squire Green" in Harborne and took every means to improve the parish — its good appearance was due to his public spirit and generosity. He was a strict Justice of the Peace, taking his duties very seriously. He caused a prison called the Round House, to be built in War Lane as a 'terror to evil-doers' as the nearest lock-up for offenders was five miles away in West Bromwich. But it proved very unpopular and was demolished one night by outraged locals, so the local village constable had once again "to shut his eyes to many offenders to save his long tramp in handcuffs" to West Bromwich, according to Presterne's book.

He founded Harborne Sunday Schools in 1794 which opened in two small cottages belonging to him. According to an account written in 1896 by a local Harborne character, "the boys' cottage was in the garden belonging to Harborne Hall and the girls were in another cottage". This appears to be the earliest evidence of Harborne Hall and is recorded in W.E. Hardwicke's *Articles on the History of Harborne.*

There is a manuscript document dated 1806-8 in Birmingham Reference Library listing all Thomas Green's property and tenants. Properties were in Harborne and Harts Green areas, including farms and other buildings, indicating he was a wealthy man.

Thomas Green died in 1803, aged 72 years, at Harborne House, his residence. There is a family memorial on the wall in St Peter's Church in Harborne which praises his "liberal and generous exertions" for the improvement of Harborne and "his active zeal in promoting the Religious Instruction of the rising generation". On his death the Lordship of the anor of Harborne and all his estates passed to his son Thomas, who, with Hannah his widow, presumably continued to live at Harborne House until her death in 1813. As Thomas had no children the estates then devolved upon his nephew Thomas Green Simcox, son of his sister Elizabeth and her husband George Simcox.

George Simcox 1763-1831

George Simcox owned a brass foundry business in Livery Street, Birmingham (which afterwards became Simcox & Pemberton, then Thomas Pemberton & Sons). His first wife was Elizabeth Green, daughter of Thomas Green. Her father built Harborne Hall for her but it is unlikely she lived long enough to enjoy it as she died in 1795, aged 32. According to St Peter's Church memorials her son George, born 1789, died at the age of 18 days but her first son, Thomas Green Simcox, survived.

George's second wife was Elizabeth Pratt, whom he married in 1796. Several of their children died young — George in 1801 aged 4, Georgiana in 1808 aged 5 and Frederick in 1808 aged 4 months. Their only surviving son was Edward George Simcox who became curate at Harborne.

George Simcox lived at Harborne Hall for many years and provided the family with a coat of arms in 1821. He was made a Justice of the Peace in 1824 in Warwickshire. He was also a governor of Birmingham's Edward VI Free Grammar School giving a published address in 1822, which is in the Birmingham Reference Library. He was a founder member of the Birmingham branch of the British and Foreign Bible Society. His monument in St Peter's Church praises his generosity.

His eldest son Thomas Green Simcox (1787-1828) was a partner in his business and lived at Harborne Hall for some time until he inherited from his uncle, Thomas Green, the Lordship of the Manor of Harborne and all his estates. He married Hannah Maria Lea in 1809 and appears to have lived mainly at Harborne House after his inheritance, according to a Simcox pedigree. His eldest son Thomas Green Simcox inherited his title and is mentioned later in this publication.

In 1831 George Simcox died at the age of 69 years, leaving his widow Elizabeth to continue to live at the Hall with her son Edward George. She died in 1843, aged 76, and occupied the Hall until this time. On the 1843 Tithe Map she was listed as owning and occupying property called The Lawns, including a house and garden which was on the site of Harborne

Hall. An 1834 map by Newey had already named the Hall and marked it on the map.

During George Simcox's occupancy of Harborne Hall the census reveals that in 1801 the parish of Harborne had a population of only 1,178. It was not until 1818 that Harborne as a village appeared in a directory, in which Simcox is listed as one of the gentry. There was at that time a Free School where one child from each poor family in the parish could be freely educated. The main street of Harborne had no pavements, surfacing or lighting. In summer it was a dustbowl and in winter an avenue of mud, deeply rutted by farm carts or horse drawn carriages. Homes were lit by oil lamps or candles. When the wells failed in hot summers water had to be carried from Moor Pool, which was also a popular place for bathing.

In 1825 the new vicar of St Peter's was Revd. James Thomas Law which was a lucky appointment for the district as he enlarged a neglected church parish and gave new impetus to a growing village. He was aided by his two curates, members of the Simcox family, Edward George Simcox (son of George) and Thomas Green Simcox (grandson of George).

Edward George Simcox 1801-1833

Edward George Simcox (son of George Simcox) continued to live at Harborne hall after his father's death in 1831, with his mother Elizabeth.

He had been educated at Oxford, obtaining a BA in 1822 and MA in 1828, and became a Justice of the Peace for Staffordshire. He was a curate at St Peter's Church Harborne where Revd. James T. Law had been Vicar since 1825. He was joined in the curacy in 1833 by his relative Thomas Green Simcox. Both of them were well remembered for their administrative talents and social influence in the parish. As Revd. Law was Chancellor of the Diocese of Lichfield and Coventry he was often absent from Harborne and relied on his curates to conduct many of the church services.

Edward was married to Charlotte Gisborne who died in 1832 aged 27, six weeks after the death of her five month old daughter Millicent. Edward himself died a year later at the age of 32 in 1833. Their only surviving son George Gisborne Simcox was orphaned at the age of five and emigrated later to Texas where he died in 1865, donating £500 to St Peter's Church.

After 1833 Elizabeth Simcox, George's widow, lived at the Hall until her death in 1843. Members of the Simcox family are mentioned at various dates in deeds on Harborne Hall up to 1883.

Thomas Green Simcox 1810-1876

Thomas Green Simcox was born at Harborne Hall on 14th March 1810, being the son of Thomas Green Simcox and grandson of George Simcox. He attended King Edward VI Grammar School in Birmingham before going to Wadham College in Oxford where he graduated with an MA in mathematics and classics. After considering a career at the bar he decided to enter the church.

In 1833 he joined Edward George Simcox, his close relative, in St Peter's Church in Harborne. He was curate there for five years under the Revd. James Law who lived mainly in Lichfield where he was Chancellor. He had

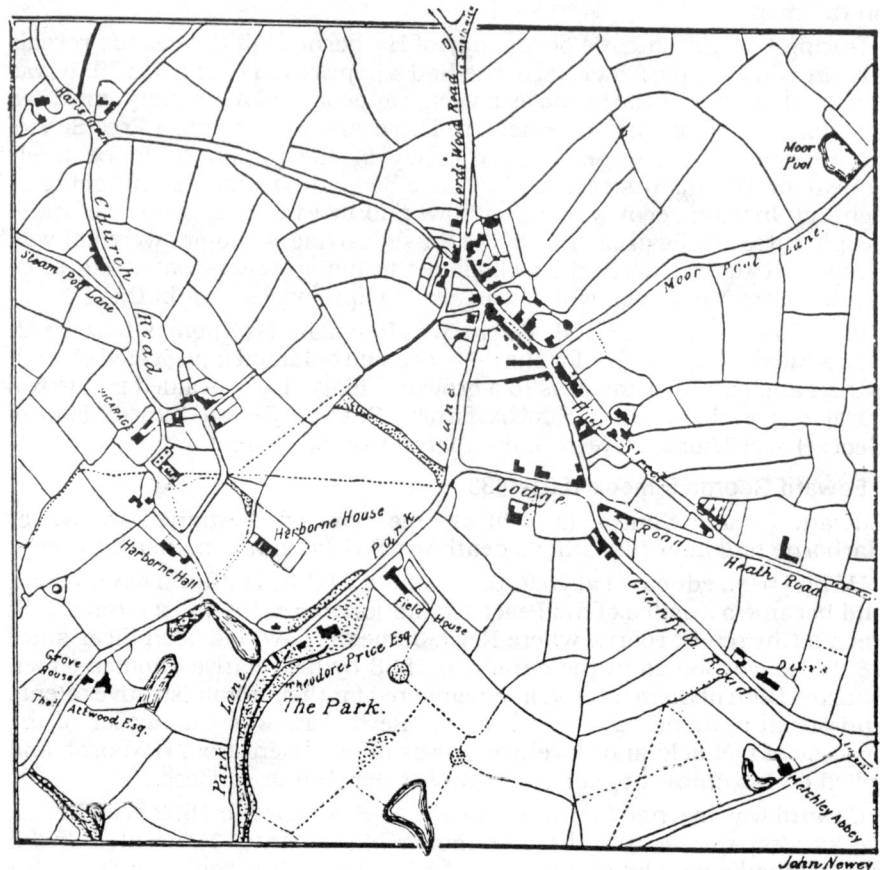

1834 map showing Harborne Hall

special responsibility for the hamlet of Smethwick, just then beginning its remarkably rapid commercial development. Smethwick at that time comprised two thirds of the parish of Harborne. A new village was developing along the canal, where Thomas Simcox was largely responsible for the building of the new church of Holy Trinity, North Harborne. He had acquired land from John Unett, contributed generously to the cost himself and was made the church's first incumbent in 1838, which he held until 1871 when ill health forced him to retire. The actual separation of the new parish from Harborne took place in 1842.

When he left Harborne parish in 1838 a silver flagon was presented to him inscribed "from his friends of Harborne". While he had been in Harborne he lived mainly at Harborne House, inherited from his father, as he was Lord of the Manor of Harborne and a wealthy man, owning much of the land in the area. A conveyance deed shows he owned Harborne Hall

The Hall in the early nineteenth century, sketched by a member of the Simcox family

with other members of the Simcox family in 1850. In 1838 he married Hannah Nicholson-Kingdon, a vicar's daughter and had three children.

In 1840 he built, at his own expense, a vicarage which he occupied for many years, opposite Holy Trinity Church. He laboured in the parish for over thirty years, according to his obituary, "playing no small part in shaping the progress and destiny of the modern borough of Smethwick". His main single desire was "to bring other to believe, fear and love God."

He had a wide charity for all, being a Guardian of the Poor in Kings Norton for many years and a founder member of the Smethwick Local Board of Health, where one of his projects was the provision of baths and wash-houses. He was much concerned with improving housing conditions in Smethwick where many dwellings were inadequately designed and poorly ventilated. On his Harborne estate he erected two model cottages in 1874 and improved tenants' living conditions. He was also keen to preserve the countryside, urging local manufacturers to reduce smoke pollution in Smethwick.

It is interesting to note that he was one of several Harborne people to sign a document in 1837 which concerned the desecration of Sunday, the Lord's Day. All who signed declared "they would not pay or receive wages nor buy or sell, nor work in the garden, collect money, travel for business or pleasure, frequent public houses nor attend Sunday games. They would avoid giving unnecessary work to servants, sending persons on errands". Their final declaration was "to keep their houses closed during the time of Divine service and to promote and attend public worship".

In 1835 Harborne was described in Dugdale's *History of England* as "a delightful village, where the cottagers are principally employed in the making of nails. There are several celebrated strawberry gardens in the

9

village, much frequented in the summer season by visitors from Birmingham".

Thomas Simcox retired to Winchester in 1871. He died at the age of 66 years and was buried in Winchester Cemetery on 23rd August 1876. He is commemorated by a brass in Holy Trinity Church, Smethwick. Being an industrious man he had a favourite saying 'Never be Idle', and in his will made provision for a clock on the church tower as a permanent memorial of his sense of time. His son, Revd. Henry Kingdon-Simcox, became Lord of the Manor of Harborne on his death but by 1908 the Lordship had passed to the Marquess of Anglesey.

Chapter 4

Harborne Hall in Victorian Times: 1837-1883

Edward Dinwoody Wilmot (1811-1884)

Edward Wilmot lived at Harborne Hall from 1850-1855 with his wife Sarah ten children and three servants (housemaid, cook and nurse). The children ranged from 4 months to 12 years — Lizzie, Jane, Mary, Nellie, John, Alice, Edith, Rose, Willy and Bertha. The last two were born at the Hall in 1850 and 1852. Edward and his wife were both listed in the census as being 39 years of age.

He was born in St Paul's Square, Birmingham — the son of John Wilmot, a metal worker and factor, who was later in business with William Roberts, another occupant of the Hall. Edward became a successful Birmingham businessman, in partnership at first with his father and William Roberts but in 1855 he branched out on his own in the wholesale jewellery business, in Hylton Street in the Jewellery Quarter. He converted domestic houses into industrial use, the frontage of which remains intact today. He travelled

Edward Dinwoody Wilmot, 1811-1884

the principal towns of the country on business and in those "coaching days few 'men of the road' were better known than he for his business aptitude and upright dealing", according to his obituary.

He must have enjoyed gracious living at Harborne Hall, with carriages, portraits and statues as he made several donations in his will to the Birmingham Art Gallery, General Dispensary and the Protestant Dissenting Charity School in Graham Street, near his business. At the school he was a subscriber, Visitor and scrutineer from 1861. Supported by voluntary subscriptions the school maintained, clothed and educated poor female children who were taught needlework, housework and other elementary matters. The main aim of the school was to enable the pupils to enter domestic service and to occupy positions in respectable households.

Edward Wilmot was one of the earliest friends of the well-known Nonconformist minister and preacher George Dawson who became a close family friend, as is shown in family letters still in existence. Edward contributed financially to the building of the Church of the Saviour, in Edward Street, in 1846-48, where Dawson became minister for thirty years.

George Dawson was an extraordinary man whose charismatic presence helped to develop Victorian Birmingham as a political community,

Sarah Barnes Wilmot, 1812-1852

12

The Church of the Saviour

advocating municipal reforms such as education for the working class, free libraries, public baths, the reformation of juvenile offenders and many social and environmental improvements. His "moral mission" was to culminate in the celebrated "civic gospel" carried out by Joseph Chamberlain, which was a new approach to municipal administration.

George Dawson, who had no specific ecclesiastical training, came to Birmingham in 1844 as a Baptist minister at Mount Zion Chapel in Graham Street. This "athletic young man of 23, with long black curly hair and clothes of a most unclerical cut" made a dramatic impact. Wright Wilson, his contemporary biographer, tells us "every available inch of room in pew, aisle and staircase was covered" for his sermons. But his unconventional views were such that the "Baptist denomination was not accustomed to recognise" and he was forced to resign after sixteen months. However, he was so popular with his congregation that they immediately set about erecting the Church of the Saviour as their place of worship, inviting Dawson to become minister.

Dawson's sermons advocated public service as a religious duty, aiming to raise the moral and intellectual standards of his fellow townsmen by active radical preaching and lecturing on many subjects. Charles Kingsley referred to him as "the best public speaker in England" — Dawson had a rare gift for speaking and teaching. According to one contemporary report he had "refined common sense, keen perception as to the capabilities of his audience and a gentle rivulet of humour which kept his hearers awake

13

George Dawson
Courtesy of The Birmingham Post

without putting too much strain upon their powers". The "union of classes" which Dawson sought was based on the Christian idea that "we are all truly one kindred and one brotherhood". He preached "a great want of our time is Unity and the present age seeks a church that shall teach the great doctrine of Brotherhood and Equality . . . swallowing up all vain distinction". He never tired of teaching that real religion should unite and not divide. His dominant conviction was that religion, the greatest of all concerns, should pervade the thoughts and actions of men in every form; that it should rule in the State, the community and the family. He believed righteousness was above dogma and trust in God was greater than all.

Dawson preached the gospel of public duty to a congregation which produced no less than seventeen town counsellors, including six mayors. Edward Wilmot was a staunch member of the congregation although he took no part in public affairs. He is portrayed in a portrait of Dawson and the Congregation of the Church of the Saviour by Ernest Thompson, which is in Birmingham Art Gallery. A large portrait of Dawson by Munns, painted in 1877, was donated by Edward Wilmot to the Art Gallery in his will.

Edward frequently moved house to accommodate his enlarging family.

One of his friends in the 1840s was David Cox, the Birmingham artist who lived nearby in Greenfield Road, Harborne. Cox was a close friend of William Roberts, Edward's brother-in-law and business partner. It is recorded in Solly's *Memoirs of David Cox* that one painting was given to Edward in exchange for half a fat pig and a silver watch. Another time David Cox wrote to William Roberts: "I cannot sufficiently return my thanks to dear Mrs Wilmot for her great kindness in sending such a bountiful present of biscuits, a hamper sufficient to feed half a dozen children for six weeks. It will give me great pleasure if you will all come to my cottage and eat raspberries and cream".

In 1852 the sad and sudden death at the Hall of his wife Sarah at the age of 40 after the birth of her tenth child, must have been a great tragedy. She was the daughter of William Freeman, a Mayor and Justice of the Peace of Norwich and had many sisters. Edward asked her younger sister Felicia to come and keep house for his large family. Two years later, in 1854, he married her abroad at Dinsberg on Rhine, it being illegal to marry a sister-in-law in England at that time. She was 16 years younger and loved to sing songs with her step daughters in the evenings. She was delicate but bore him three sons before she also died at the young age of 31, at the family's next residence at Key Hill House in Hockley, near the Jewellery Quarter. As the family had increased to thirteen, including a governess, Edward persuaded another sister-in-law, Phoebe, to come and help him. He married her six months later in 1859, in Switzerland this time. At the age of 34 she bore her first child with difficulty, but went on to have another six children, although two died in infancy, a common occurrence in those times. Letters from Edward's eldest daughter, Jane, reveal a fascinating glimpse into the large family of young children. Jane had great sympathy with motherless children, after having lost her own mother at the age of 12 years and gave lessons to the girls at home. One of the boys went to George Dawson's wife's school in Bromsgrove, boarding there from 1861.

Phoebe Wilmot, who was fourteen years younger than her husband, leaves a fascinating account of life in such a large household, in letters to her sister-in-law in Norwich. There must have been many problems in running such a household which she compared with "a beehive, each bee with its own work to do and everything in an uproar if any girls neglect their duties". She was destined to have ten of the girls at home for many years until they married. Florence Nightingale Freeman Wilmot, one of her own children, remained unmarried and became an artist. Letters mention the lovely autumn trees around their home which several of the girls painted. However, the only painting of Harborne Hall that exists was painted by Mary Jane Roberts, Edward's niece.

All the children were taken annually to the dentist by horse and carriage. One of the girls, Rose, hated the event and hid up a tree while all the other girls were dressed up in muslin frocks with coloured silk sashes and hats. After the carriage had departed she climbed down and ran round to the kitchen where a sympathetic cook offered her some tarts and a cup of milk. History does not relate the consequences but it was ironic she suffered with her teeth all her life. It is interesting to note that there were thirty-four years between Edward Wilmot's first and last child.

During Edward Wilmot's residence at the Hall communications began to improve as the postal service had started in 1844. A horse bus called "Noah's Ark" became well established being a vehicle of capacious dimensions, taking an hour to get to Birmingham for the sum of six pence. It was referred to as "the village gossip shop and debating society combined".

There would have been no gas supply in the 1850s. Water was still supplied by spring or pump — in Birmingham citizens were still accustomed to buying water supplies from water carriers. Harborne Hall had a spring in the grounds which fed the Pool in Grove Park. In the village of Harborne there were open sewers which were usually overflowing and covered in slime.

The local cottage industry was nail making which gave farm labourers a winter income until the industry became mechanised a few years later. Other local industries were iron and glass. Entertainments locally included bull baiting down at the King's Arms.

A nearby neighbour at Grove House was Thomas Attwood, Birmingham's first Member of Parliament and a banker. He was a champion of reform and founder of political unions for the middle working class. The main landowner in Harborne was the Revd. T.G. Simcox, Lord of the Manor of Harborne.

Edward Wilmot died on 14th October 1884 at the age of 73, at Ashley House in Handsworth and was buried in the Victorian Non-conformist Cemetery at Key Hill in the Jewellery Quarter, with his first two wives, his parents and three of his children. His third wife, Phoebe, rests alone in Mickleton Churchyard in the Cotswolds, perhaps enjoying the peace she never found in running a home for all her husband's twenty children.

William Roberts (1788-1867)

William Roberts came to the Hall in his retirement from 1856-67, with his wife Mary Jane (Edward Wilmot's sister), his two "lovely" daughters Mary and Sarah, his nephew John Roberts and two house servants. The house was leased from Howard Simcox.

He was a Yorkshire man, born at Darton, spending most of his business life in Birmingham where he was in partnership with John Wilmot from 1818 at St Mary's Row and Summer Row as a "merchant and factor". The firm Wilmot & Roberts "stood as high as any in public estimation", according to his obituary, probably selling goods which had been manufactured by John Wilmot, a metal worker. John Wilmot had come from St Paul's Square where he had advertised "all kinds of fire irons in steel, iron, plated with silver or imperial metal, standards, grate heads and ornaments of every description". John Wilmot died in 1840 so William Roberts carried on successfully on his own until he entered into partnership with Edward Wilmot, the son. Edward branched out on his own in the business about 1855, probably at the time when William Roberts retired.

16

William Roberts was an amateur artist of some repute, having always painted since his youth. Through his business pursuits in Norwich he formed a friendship with several artists of the Norwich School of Art, including John Crome and John Cotman. He also studied under another artist, Peter de Wint. His abilities as an artist developed through these contacts and he was well known for narrating amusing anecdotes to his artistic friends. He was also a collector of paintings and patron of the arts, contributing to the first exhibition of paintings in 1819 at the Birmingham Academy of Arts.

He became an expert in oil painting, was deeply interested in the materials of painting and had a great influence on the artist David Cox who learned the technique of using oils from him. In a letter dated 1841 David Cox expressed his gratitude to William Roberts for the assistance he gave "in acquiring some knowledge in the delightful branch of the arts, oil painting". Cox moved from London to Harborne, settling in Greenfield House, in order to be near his friend William Roberts. Cox's friendship had a powerful influence on William's artistic style; both men produced similar pictures "with a broad and grand view of nature" on their many painting expeditions together. Their paintings

David Cox

are frequently mistaken for each other's. Haddon Hall was a favourite spot, also the immediate neighbourhood of Harborne. They loved the ever changing leafy foliage and beautiful lanes and countryside of Harborne — "fine trees, rural cottages, country people at their wicket gates or driving home the cows or porkers" were all favourite subjects. David Cox's home had a view of meadows and open country towards Hagley which provided many views for his sketches. William Roberts' daughter Mary painted Harborne Hall in 1867, which survives today.

David Cox was known to his friends and neighbours as "old farmer Cox" or "dear old David Cox" and he was not really appreciated by the world for his art until after his death. He had another close friend, Charles Birch, living at Metchley Abbey, who was a great authority and collector of pictures. He was the friendly medium between Cox and wealthy patrons of art. Roberts, Cox and Birch were known as "fast companions, a trio of fine old English gentlemen" spending their time convivially together. After the death of his wife Cox spent his Christmas Day with William Roberts or Charles Birch until his own death in 1859, where William was one of the pall-bearers at his funeral. There is a window commemorating Cox in St Peter's Church.

In a biography on Cox by N. Solly there are several incidents mentioning William Roberts and the Wilmots. A Miss Wilmot was given the choice of purchasing one of his paintings for £5 in preference to Roberts or Birch who were willing to pay £15 for this painting. Another painting, Crossing Lancaster Sands, a celebrated picture full of atmospheric effect and beautiful in colour, was given to Mr Wilmot in exchange for half a pig.

William Roberts died at the age of 79 years on 26th March 1867 and is buried in St Peter's Churchyard alongside his old friend David Cox, although his gravestone is unreadable, in comparison with Cox's which is still very clear. It was said William Roberts could have attained a high and distinguished position as an artist but chose instead to be a successful businessman. However, he will be remembered for his attachment to the fine arts and his skill as an artist — Birmingham Art Gallery has several of his paintings and sketches which are a fine memorial.

Charles Hart (1820-1880)

Charles Hart took up residence at the Hall in 1868 at the age of 48, living there for twelve years until his death. In 1871 the census reveals he lived with his son Charles (19, architectural student), son George (18, medical student), his sister, sister-in-law, domestic cook, housemaid and groom. His wife was not listed, and he was described as "iron and scrap founder".

He had moved from London when his metal work business branched out at a new factory at Grosvenor Street, Birmingham, as the original premises had been acquired by London Council for the building of a new road. His firm, Messrs Hart & Son, ecclesiastical metalworkers, had been established in London by his father in 1816. Charles Hart acquired new showrooms in Charing Cross Road and all the manufacturing was moved up to Birmingham after 1867.

The company was famous throughout the country for its artistic iron work and brass work, varying from massive structures such as wrought iron gates for Hampton Court Palace, to delicate silver chalices and altar crosses. Many church ornaments were made in hammered silver, also electric light fittings at a later date. The firm later became Messrs Hart, Son, Peard & Co. which provided items for many churches, cathedrals and public buildings throughout the country. Birmingham has many examples of the firm's work including gates, brasses and railings in St Martin's Church, brass work and balconies in the Council House and items in the

General Hospital, Town Hall, old Reference Library, University and Victoria Law Courts.

Charles Hart was a generous patron of St Peter's Church, Harborne and presented a beautiful brass eagle lectern as a gift in 1874 in memory of his third son Frank. In his first year at Harborne Hall he donated the lych gate nearest the Hall to St Peter's, made by his firm. There is a carving on the crossbeam: "gift of Charles Hart".

He made extensive alterations to the Hall while in residence, commissioning John Henry Chamberlain, the Birmingham architect. (A sample of his work from nearby Grove House is on display at the Victoria & Albert Museum — a complete room, with panelling and contents, called "The Harborne Room"). The Hall is rich in decorations and mouldings of the nineteenth century.

In 1872 he was on the committee of the Council for Education and voted for the erection of a new Infants School, according to the provisions of the 1870 Act for Elementary Education. He was one of several benefactors to the charity of Harborne National Society School Scheme which entitled him to become one of the first 'non-official' managers to inspect the school. The school's main aim was "to promote the education of the poor in the principles of the Established Church".

1874 was a celebrated year for Harborne as the first railway to Birmingham was opened. The first train decorated with red, green and white flags left the station on 10th August for Birmingham, the third class fare being 4½d. for the twenty-five minute journey. The Harborne railway became of a legend — not for nothing was it known as the Harborne Express.

Another record was created in 1875 when a local man, James Barton, grew the largest gooseberry in England, being a member of the local Gooseberry Grower's Society which had been formed in 1815.

On 17th January 1880 Charles Hart suddenly died at the age of 60 after visiting London. He was seized with an attack of broncho-pneumonia to which he succumbed after two days, according to his obituary. Although he was retiring by nature with a quiet and unostentatious manner his twelve years residence in Harborne had been noted for his acts of charity and good counsel. His gifts to religious and educational institutions had been considerable. He is buried in Harborne churchyard, not far from the gate which he donated to St Peter's Church.

Charles Joseph Hart (1851-1925)

Charles Joseph Hart came to the Hall in 1868 with his father Charles Hart, as a young man of 17 years and lived there until 1883.

He became a well know figure in the Birmingham area as head of his art metalwork business of Messrs Hart, Son, Peard & Co. and as a popular Volunteer officer in First Volunteer Battalion of Royal Warwickshire Regiment, leading a most active life. In the 1881 census he was 29 years of age, an art metal worker born in Surrey, living at Harborne Hall with his sister Helen (23), brother Albert (18), a cook and a parlour maid. The coachman and his wife, with a domestic servant, were living at the Hall Lodge.

In his first year at Harborne Hall he enrolled as a private in the First Warwickshire Rifle Volunteers which in 1883 became the First Volunteer Battalion of Royal Warwickshire Regiment. He became Captain in 1875 and Honorary Major in 1886, going on to be promoted to Honorary Lieutenant Colonel in 1894. He was in the first list of officers to whom the Volunteer Decoration was given for twenty years service. In 1901 he became Colonel of the First Volunteer Battalion and during World War I he had the distinction of enlisting over 80,000 men as Birmingham's Recruiting Officer. He also acted as the Military Authority for the sale and manufacture

Illustration from an 1875 trade catalogue of Hart & Son

of arms and ammunition. In 1919 he was made a Commander with the Military Division of the Order of the British Empire having had a remarkable service record of over fifty years in the auxiliary services. Another honour was conferred on him by the King of the Belgians in 1921 — *Officier de l'Ordre de la Couronne.*

He was the pioneer of route marching in the Midlands — the first one took place in 1885 which was a tremendous success. In 1895/6 he used

Charles J. Hart, 1851–1925

21

the land west of Harborne church for night time marches. A contemporary report states: "so stealthily was the march conducted that the special police on duty in the vicinity of the church had no idea of the presence of the Volunteers until close upon them. Having accomplished the object of the march, at Harborne the restrictions were withdrawn and headed by the bugle band, the battalions made a triumphant passage through Harborne on the return journey to headquarters".

He was expert in the study of military tactics, passing the first examination in the subject in 1882. He published a booklet *How the War Game is Played*, articles in the *Birmingham Daily Post* on regimental events and a book on the history of the regiment in 1906 which is a fascinating account. In the book he mentions how he sought the support of Joseph Chamberlain to raise funds for Volunteers and how his regiment headed the Queen's Diamond Jubilee procession in Birmingham in 1897. He was presented with a special certificate of thanks for his help in the Jubilee Celebrations by the Lord Mayor.

He also gives an account in the book of Jack, their battalion mascot, which had joined the regiment from the Boers in South Africa, to become one of the best known dogs in Birmingham. (Jack died in 1908 — his head was stuffed for regimental officers and his pads formed handles for paperknives.)

There are many news cut-

BIRMINGHAM VOLUNTEER,
1885.
(FIRST VOLUNTEER BATTALION ROYAL WARWICK-
SHIRE REGIMENT).

The uniform of the Birmingham Volunteers

tings mentioning Charles Hart in the St John's Royal Warwickshire Regimental Museum in Warwick, which are too numerous to relate here. He turned to soldiering as a relaxation and was a very humane officer. Probably only a bachelor would have been allowed to devote some twenty or thirty Saturday evenings each year to volunteering. He was never happier than when planning some drill, organising a parade or leading back to camp the troops he had directed throughout the day, according to one contemporary news cutting.

His other interests included shooting competitions, golf and archaeology. Being a member of Birmingham Archaeological Society he wrote several articles in 1893/4 and 1903 on "old iron work", "old chests" (illustrated by himself) and "antiquity of iron". Locally in Harborne he was on the first committee for the Harborne & Edgbaston Institute which was opened in 1878 — his name is on a wall plaque. Popular lectures, social gatherings and entertainments were its purpose.

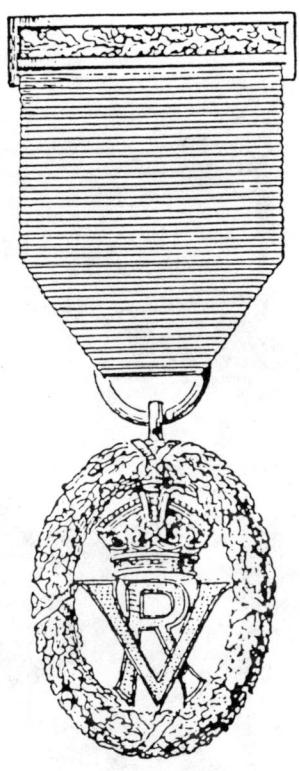

The Volunteer Decoration — the long service medal awarded to Charles Joseph Hart.

He was most well known in Harborne as being the founder of Harborne Volunteer Fire Brigade with his brother George in 1879, being its first Captain. It operated with two officers, a foreman and six firemen, having but 600 feet of canvas hose and 80 feet of leather. In a letter from Harborne Hall, dated 17th March 1881, he appealed to local residents for donations to purchase a "manual engine" as the existing appliance had repeatedly proved inefficient. Over £190 was raised which provided an engine, accessories and uniform and fitted out premises in Serpentine Road as a fire station. By 1883 the brigade was dealing with seven fires a year, in each case getting away with the engine or hose cart, horsed within five minutes of the alarm. On leaving Harborne that year his contribution to the Brigade was acknowledged at a public dinner given in his honour when he was presented with an illuminated address.

He directed much energy to developing his art metalwork business and led fellow manufacturers in matters of encouraging the application of art

In 1903 the firm of Hart, Son, Peard & Co. made the column of this Chamberlain clock in the Birmingham Jewellery Quarter

principles to industrial production. Many notable productions were made for a multitude of buildings and places by his firm. In 1903 his business had the honour of making the column of one of the "Chamberlain clocks", a clock in Vyse Street in the Birmingham Jewellery Quarter, commemorating Joseph Chamberlain's visit to South Africa as Secretary of State for the Colonies in 1903. It was unveiled by Mary Chamberlain, the politician's wife, being erected by Chamberlain's constituents of West Birmingham, by public subscription. It included a quotation from a speech, "We have shown we can be strong and resolute in war; it is equally important to show we can be resolute and strong in peace". In 1989 the clock was in danger of collapsing and was renovated in 1990 at a cost of £106,000, with electric lamps replacing the original ones which were of the candelabra type. It stands proudly in Warstone Lane on its island and is a fine sight.

Examples of the artistic hammered ironwork produced by his firm were donated to the Birmingham Art Gallery after the close of the 1886 British Association Bingley Hall Exhibition for local industry. He was presented by the exhibitors with an illuminated address as a token of his contribution to the very successful event he had organised.

His most important public work, apart from Volunteering, was in connection with the Birmingham School of Art, where he recognised the importance of art in industry, being on the Committee for many years. This led to the institution being judged a model school of art, where he gave many lectures. He had also studied architecture as a young man and was a President of the Midlands Arts Club.

In 1902 he was made a Justice of the Peace for Warwickshire, sitting at Aston. He retired to Leamington Spa in 1920 to live at "Southbank" by the river and was a member of the Milverton bench of magistrates. He died at the age of 73 on 4th March 1925 after a lengthy illness and was buried in Harborne.

Dr George Hart

Dr George Hart was the second son of Charles Hart, born about 1853, having moved with him from London in 1868. He lived at Harborne Hall, listed as a medical student in the 1871 census. He probably lived there until 1875 when he was registered as a doctor, a member of the Royal College of Surgeons, practising at Green Road, Harborne and later Heath Road. He became Assistant House Surgeon at the Birmingham General Hospital, Summer Lane.

He was also a Volunteer and a member of the Salvation Army when it was formed in 1882. He was a member or speaker of the Harborne Young Men's Friendly Society, a movement founded in 1885 "to establish the healthy recreation of young men and to promote moral well being". Dr Hart was an enthusiastic photographer and gave a talk in 1889 which was "very memorable" according to a contemporary report. He described the process of taking photographs as very slow, occupying some 20-30 minutes. During the evening he photographed the Chairman, Revd. E Roberts, in a "flash of artificial lighting produced by gun-cotton and magnesium powder". His interest in photography resulted in a large collection of photographs and lantern slides on "old Harborne", started in 1893 when the society purchased a magic lantern. His collection was still in use in 1940.

He was known locally as being a founder member of Harborne Volunteer Fire Brigade and took over the captaincy after his brother Charles resigned. His 1888 annual report states that the brigade headed the Jubilee procession that year and was inspected by Queen Victoria at Windsor in June 1888. In 1891 the brigade was disbanded when it was taken over by the Birmingham authority.

Bertram (Albert) E. Hart

Bertram Hart was born about 1863, the youngest of the four brothers. He lived at Harborne Hall from 1868 until at least 1881, when he was recorded in the census as a science student. He joined the Volunteers in 1880, later becoming a Major. He had a great interest in shooting competitions and also identified strongly with the Church Lads' Brigade, starting a company at Selly Oak.

Chapter 5

Extensions to Harborne Hall: 1884-1901

Walter Chamberlain lived at Harborne Hall from 1885-1902, after he had been on world travels. He was the youngest son of Joseph Chamberlain who had founded the successful screw making business of Nettlefold & Chamberlain in 1854 with John Sutton Nettlefold, using newly invented machinery. Walter's elder brother Joseph (who became the well known Birmingham politician and statesman) had worked in the family business showing such flair and initiative that the firm had become one of Birmingham's leading screw manufacturers. Walter entered the business at the age of 18, spent two years going through the workshops and drawing office and eventually became the foreman and manager of the fitting shop. He became chief engineer at the Heath Street works and also managed the Kings Norton works. The firm set a good example of management, with great emphasis on the health and welfare of employees, in contrast with many competitors.

In 1874 the Chamberlains sold their share of the business as Joseph had become Mayor Birmingham in 1873, becoming one of the city's great "municipal reformers", a realisation of George Dawson's prophesies. Dawson himself had persuaded Joseph to stand for the Town Council. Walter and his brother Herbert also left the firm, the sale of the business providing the Chamberlains with a substantial fortune. Walter was presented with a testimonial in the form of a handsome inscribed solid silver centre-piece for flowers from the Smethwick workers "as a token of their admiration of his character and abilities". In his speech he spoke of the "willing service which had always been rendered to him as manager and the kindly feeling entertained towards him". To commemorate their departure from the business the Chamberlains organised an enormous works outing. Almost 1000 employees and their wives were taken by special trains to London to visit Crystal Palace. Tea and a three course dinner were provided which was an act of generosity remembered for a long time.

Walter retired temporarily from business in 1875 on the proceeds of the business sale, embarking on a world tour with his brother Herbert. He met and married *en route* a Canadian girl in Montreal, called Agnes Gilmour, "one of the fairest and most estimable young ladies of Canadian society". He travelled the world for five years with his wife, visiting Ceylon, the Far East, Australia, New Zealand, Canada, the United States and some Pacific Islands, acquiring a South Sea island during this time. In 1881 he set off on another series of travels and also visited India in 1885. Then he returned to a business career and purchased Harborne Hall as a home.

All the Chamberlain brothers had large houses in Joseph's constituency of West Birmingham which included Harborne, Joseph's residence being Highbury.

In 1884 the firm of architects Martin and Chamberlain more than doubled the size of the stucco faced classical house. There was some criticism that

Walter Chamberlain, 1847–1920

Martin and Chamberlain's alterations and additions were 'unforgivably uncompromising', with the new stone bay window to the drawing room being 'entirely out of scale with the earlier work', according to an account of the architects plans in a publication in Bishop's Croft. Unfortunately the original plans cannot be traced.

The original building of Harborne Hall had been L-shaped, consisting of a living range facing south with a service wing at its western end projecting towards the north. The main entrance, a Tuscan porch, survived to serve its original purpose but the north side of the main range beyond was demolished to make way for considerable extensions.

The exterior became a mixture of classical and Gothic. There are stained glass windows on the first floor with the Lion and Key crest of Walter Chamberlain. The crest is repeated in the carvings of the staircase newels in the main hall with his motto *"Je Tiens Ferme"*, and on the balcony are beautiful floral carvings. The impressive hall is very similar to Joseph Chamberlain's hall at Highbury which had been designed by J.H. Chamberlain of the same firm of architects. Exotic art is evident in many aspects of the Hall, including the panelled entrance in the drawing room, where gilt palm trees and birds are silhouetted against a black lacquer background, framed by Gothic arches. There is a splendid billiard room with a continuous terra-cotta frieze of plants. The glass in the porch is richly coloured with cornflowers and peonies, and the front oak door has two panels filled with delicate carvings of birds and plants. In the vestibule are varnished wooden screens with painted glass panels depicting oak, holly, mistletoe, thistle and various birds. The view southwest from the Hall was at one time completely rural.

1870s advertisement for the French market

Walter and Agnes Chamberlain had three children — Herbert (known to the family as Bertie), Basil and Pearl. Herbert died of appendicitis while a pupil at Rugby. Basil served as Captain in the Worcestershire Yeomanry, being awarded the Military Cross and was a prisoner of war in Turkey for two and a half years. His sister Pearl served in the First World War as a nurse in the V.A.D. (Voluntary Aid Detachment) movement. She had been born at Harborne Hall and christened at St Peter's Church in a thunderstorm. The servants were also at the ceremony which was quite a fashionable gathering, according to a contemporary news cutting. The christening cake had been made by the housekeeper and was quite a work of art, with a twist of smilax round it grown by the head gardener. The family and their circle of friends were very keen on amateur dramatics which is shown in a photograph depicting Walter, Agnes and Bertie in seventeenth century German costume.

In the New Year of 1889 Walter held a large dinner in honour of his brother Joseph's new bride, the American Mary Endicott, who was half his age, his third wife and the daughter of the Secretary of War. In a letter home, preserved in the Chamberlain Archives at Birmingham University, she wrote that "the Hall was very pretty, decorated with evergreen and the first thing which greeted my sight was the American flag. When we entered the room the music struck up the wedding march we had heard seven weeks

Agnes Chamberlain, wife of Walter Chamberlain, 1892

before in Washington . . . Walter took me in. I wore my green silk dress and in my hair was Papa's crescent — around my throat the pearl necklace and opal bracelet brought with my legacy . . . The shade of the stones harmonised beautifully with the green and yellow of the dress". It may be added this dinner was an eight course meal with the menu written out in French. As Walter was resident at Harborne Hall by 1885 it can be assumed the dinner was held there.

Basil and Pearl Chamberlain, 1899

Walter Chamberlain was a brilliant man with great charm and an excellent conversationalist. He was fascinated by new inventions and owned some of the earliest cars. He also had one of the first X-ray sets with which he practised on his butler in the cellar! He collected china, grew orchids, had a small zoo and was very fond of hunting, as well as being the most athletic member of his family.

A carpenter from the Hall recalls that during Walter's residence there were "penguins on the pool tame enough to take fish from one's hand" and inside the Hall were heads of deer, stuffed birds, butterflies and eggs (some were donated to Birmingham Museum). Walter Chamberlain was an enthusiastic ornithologist and had quite a large aviary which absorbed a good deal of his time. Some family photographs show some of the animals and birds on the estate as well as the horses which he used for hunting. His wife Agnes is pictured riding side-saddle on a horse which is leaping high above a fence. His coachman was known for his habit of galloping the carriage horses round the Hillyfields before putting them into harness, in order to calm them before a journey.

Walter Chamberlain's sister Mary was married to William Kenrick who rebuilt neighbouring Grove House, employing John Henry Chamberlain, the architect. A small gate was made in the Grove fence opposite Harborne Hall's entrance, no doubt for the convenience of family visits.

During his years at Harborne Walter became involved with local affairs even before his residence at the Hall. In 1874 he was the first chairman of Harborne Board School, which took over the Old British School in York Road, then opened the first new Board School in 1881. This continued until

Joseph Chamberlain and his wife Mary
after their marriage in 1888

Hulton Picture Library

1891, then Birmingham took it over as Harborne became part of Birmingham Municipal Borough.

He had little interest in politics although had once stood as a Liberal in local parliamentary elections and was also President of Harborne Liberal Unionist Association. He was primarily an astute businessman being chairman and director of many Birmingham companies such as Guest, Keen and Nettlefold, W. & T. Avery Ltd., The Soho Trust, Charles Churchill & Co., Joseph Lucas Ltd. and Central Insurance Co. He had the Chamberlain gift of 'direct, forceful utterance and was an ideal courteous chairman' according to a contemporary report. 'He possessed all the lucidity which characterises the Chamberlain family' said a colleague on the Avery Board.

In 1891 he became a director of W. & T. Avery Ltd., a firm specialising in weighing machines. William Avery had invented many improvements in weighing apparatus and was mainly responsible for the passing of the Weights & Measures Act 1889. In 1894 the firm was registered as a Public Company, in which Walter was a director. He succeeded William Avery as Chairman in 1899 and was largely responsible for the purchase of Soho Foundry and personally superintended the rebuilding works. He had 'an extraordinary knowledge of the details of business' and always showed great interest in the welfare of employees. The firm regarded their employees as a family, knowing all personally. In cases of illness it was not unknown for a carriage and horses to draw up to a worker's cottage, leaving eggs, fruit and most of all a personal touch of interest. In 1900 the firm made the largest weigh-bridge ever built at that time, 100 tons capacity. Much of the progress made at W. & T. Avery Ltd was due to Walter Chamberlain's skilful efforts in developing its operations and increasing its prosperity, right up to the time of his death.

He left the Hall in 1902 for the warmer climate in Surrey, moving to Peacock Grove, Cobham. He still kept on Harborne Hall and allowed Avery employees to use it for recreation purposes, also loaning it to Belgian refugees. The Hall was also used as a military hospital. Edward Nettlefold's residence at the Hall must have been due to his family and business connections. Walter Chamberlain died on the 25th August 1920 in Cobham. After a funeral service there he was buried at Harborne on the 30th August, being the last surviving brother of Joseph Chamberlain. His interment at Harborne was kept very secret — a number of beautiful wreaths were sent to Cobham by mistake. Some of the floral tributes reflected Walter Chamberlain's sporting interests, consisting of heather, ling and gorse.

Chapter 6
Edwardian Times: 1902-1909

Edward Nettlefold (1856-1909)

Edward Nettlefold lived at Harborne Hall from 1902 to 1909, leased from Walter Chamberlain. At the time of his residence his eldest son Edward John, born 1886, would have been about 17 years old, (he joined the 5th Dragoon Guards in 1908). His other three children were Katherine, born 1888, Joseph born 1889 and Mildred born 1894. His wife was Clara Grace Hutton of Chislehurst, Kent, who lived long after his death until 1957, to the age of 93 years. He died at the Hall in 1909. The family coat of arms was granted in 1866 to Frederick Nettlefold and other descendants of John Sutton Nettlefold.

Edward was born in London, being the eldest son of Edward John Nettlefold and grandson of John Sutton Nettlefold, the founder of J.S. Nettlefold & Sons and Nettlefolds & Chamberlain. Both firms dominated the British screw market and Nettlefolds became the world's premier screw manufacturer. His father was chairman of the firm from 1866-1878 until his death.

Edward was educated at Cambridge University where he obtained a BA in 1879 and a reputation as a powerful oarsman on the river. He was a reserve for the Cambridge crew in one of the Oxford and Cambridge contests. After his MA degree he joined his father in the Nettlefolds business. He was elected to the board in 1881 on the death of his uncle Joseph H. Nettlefold (who donated to Birmingham Art Gallery his large collection of paintings by David Cox). He became Deputy Chairman from 1891-1902 and took an active part in negotiations which led to the firm amalgamating to become Guest, Keen and Nettlefold (GKN). He was a director up to the time of his death. He had also worked closely with Joseph Chamberlain, Walter's brother, on the board of Nettlefold & Chamberlain.

In the family business of Nettlefold he had been chiefly concerned with the management of the Heath Street mills in Smethwick. Conditions for the workers were 7am to 6pm, with thirty minutes for breakfast and an hour for lunch. Holidays were limited to five and a half days a year and a further day for the works outing. The firm maintained a powerful loyalty among its employees and provided many generous facilities for recreation.

He was also prominently connected with other commercial enterprises such as Lloyds Bank, Birmingham Canal Navigation Co. and the London & North Western Railway Co., where he was instrumental in obtaining considerable improvements in the train services between Birmingham and London. He took great interest in Birmingham's Agricultural Society, being a member of the Council of the Birmingham Agricultural Exhibition Society and was also involved with the Cattle and Dog Shows.

He took an active part in political and public life, being an ardent Unionist and became treasurer of the Midland Liberal Unionist Association. He was a close associate and friend of his political cousin, Joseph Chamberlain, and contributed to his cause of Tariff Reform, being a member of the Imperial Tariff Commission. He was chosen chairman of the great Unionist banquet in honour of the triumphant return of the seven Birmingham Parliamentary representatives in the 1906 General Election and gave a memorable speech, in place of Joseph Chamberlain who was laid low with an attack of influenza. He was also a Justice of the Peace for Staffordshire.

Another member of the family, Councillor J.S. Nettlefold, had a business enterprise which benefited Harborne in 1908, with "Harborne Tenants Ltd" — a model planned housing development. House owners shared part of the

Edward Nettlefold, 1856–1909

capital which was a new concept, the plan having special regard to the environment with tree planted roads, grassy areas, playgrounds and tennis courts, which were of the best examples of contemporary Birmingham. Harborne was, at that time, in danger of being too popular for building development after its amalgamation with Birmingham in 1891.

He died on 11th April 1909 at the age of 54 years after a prolonged illness, following an attack of pneumonia three years earlier. His funeral took place in Harborne and his ashes were buried in the churchyard. After his death it appears from directories that the Hall stood empty until the outbreak of the First World War in 1914.

Clara Grace Nettlefold, 1863–1957

35

Chapter 7

First World War: 1914-1918

Belgian Refugees (1914-1916)

Between the years 1914-1916 the war gave the empty Hall a new lease of life, thanks to the generosity of Walter Chamberlain who loaned the Hall to be run as a home for Belgian refugees.

A committee of dedicated people met on 12th September 1914 to decide how to prepare the place for the refugees. Their aim was to furnish and prepare the Hall in about a week, with no specific funds to finance the operation. Gifts of all kinds — furniture, clothing and household goods — poured in, in an almost ceaseless stream. The committee learned how to put up iron beds, to lay carpets and to hang curtains in time for the arrival of the first party of weary refugees on 19th September. The home was pleasant and welcoming, a good tea was ready and beds were prepared with flowers in all the principal rooms. The sad eyes of their guests soon began to brighten at the warm welcome.

A group of refugee nuns from an Antwerp convent undertook the management of the Hall under the leadership of their Superior, Mother Josepha. The stores and provisions remained in the hands of the committee. By October 1914 there were ninety-two refugees, including forty children. A constant stream of eagerly interested visitors and offers of kind hospitality and entertainment flooded in at first so that the refugees almost became blasé and indifferent.

Work was found for some of the men who contributed one third of their earnings to the home. Two babies were born during the winter but only one survived. The children were taught at the Hall by one of the nuns. Free medical assistance was given by a local doctor.

As public interest began to wane a year later and gifts and financial assistance declined, only regular subscriptions kept the home solvent.

In August 1915 the nuns returned to Belgium to take charge of their convent again, at a time when military authorities wanted to take over the Hall as a V.A.D. (Voluntary Aid Detachment) Hospital. As there were only forty-five refugees left, all were eventually found new homes. The furniture was reclaimed by the donors or kept for the hospital. The committee later received a letter signed "your devoted refugees", thanking them for the kindness and great generosity; "You have not spared yourselves any trouble, nothing has been too much for you to do, to render our life as agreeable as possible during this unhappy year of the war. It is with great regret we had to leave the hospitable dwelling of Harborne Hall which has sheltered us in our exile. We thank you a thousand times".

Harborne Hall as a V.A.D. Auxiliary Hospital (1916-1918)

In January 1916 Walter Chamberlain generously allowed his beautiful residence to be used as a military hospital for the large number of wounded

Harborne Hall auxiliary hospital, 1916–18. The annexe ward

soldiers being sent back from France. It was entirely financed by the employees of W. & T. Avery Ltd. — the firm Chamberlain had been associated with for so many years.

The Hall was redecorated, with extra small huts and marquees being erected to provide additional accommodation for the large numbers of wounded men arriving for treatment. A new ward was erected (a wooden building containing twenty-six beds together with a fully equipped operating table) and also a large dining hall catering for 200 people (with a commodious kitchen) was built in the grounds. In the kitchen garden convalescent patients helped to rear pigs and vegetables.

The hospital staff consisted mainly of voluntary workers, some of whom had earlier worked in Hill Crest Hospital, Edgbaston. At its inauguration the Hall contained 100 beds but was enlarged subsequently to accommodate up to 240 beds. Over 5,600 patients were admitted, including many colonials and allies who could not speak a word of English. All spoke gratefully of the kind treatment received at the Hospital.

The hospital was run by Mrs Heaton, the Commandant, who devoted the whole of her time to the work, being awarded an OBE in 1918 for her services. There were also a matron, a doctor and many nurses. All laundry work was carried out and financed by Mrs Conway Lowe, ably assisted by parties of lady voluntary workers. A modern dispensary for medicines was included.

In the main entrance of the Hall the overhanging balcony was draped with the Union Jack and was used for concerts, whist drives and other entertainments. A billiard table at the far end was very popular.

A committee composed of representatives from W. & T. Avery Ltd. met periodically to discuss administrative and financial matters, the chairman being Mr Cannell of the firm who devoted much time to the hospital. Additional funds came from the Newfoundland Government who sent yearly contributions and many individual people. An ambulance was lent and an Austin car as the hospital was rather inaccessible at that time.

The charm and peace of Harborne Hall must have been soothing "to heroes who had recently passed through a nerve shattering ordeal", quotes W. & T. Avery Ltd.'s special album of the hospital. The tennis court and the rose garden were favourite spots for nurses and patients — many romances flourished when local young ladies visited patients, enjoying the grounds which included a picturesque pool and an undulating country view stretching away for miles.

It took two years to deal with the patients many of them going to new homes or other hospitals, or sadly, dying. But the "Avery Hospital" became well know for many years in many parts of the world in that short time and soldiers had good cause to be very grateful to Walter Chamberlain, the voluntary staff of Harborne Hall and the employees of W. & T. Avery Ltd. The Avery Historical Museum has a unique record and set of photographs relating to this period of history of Harborne Hall.

Harborne Hall auxiliary hospital, 1916–18. View from the lawn showing nurses and patients

Chapter 8

Harborne Hall in the Twentieth Century: 1919-1991

Harborne Hall Preparatory School For Boys 1919-1924

When the First World War ended and life began to return to normal the Hall assumed a new role as a preparatory school in December 1919. It was leased to Monatagu Lawson, the headmaster, previously from Edgbaston West House School. He had a small staff of graduate teachers including his brother and catered for thirty-six pupils when the school opened. For the convenience of pupils residing in Moseley and Kings Heath there were special buses to the school for the first year but it later became a boarding school.

It boasted one of the "most completely equipped boarding schools in the Midlands with commanding views of the surrounding country including the Clent and Lickey Hills". It included, in its 37 acres of grounds, a fine reception room, dormitories, dining rooms, music room, library, music and playrooms. It had a sanatorium, chapel, carpenter's shop, gymnasium, rifle range, natural history museum, laboratory, drawing studio, photographic room and school farm supplying dairy produce. Sports included cricket, football, tennis, golf, swimming, paper chases, shooting, boxing and riding for the cost of 100 guineas per year for boarders.

The aim of the school was "to afford sound education on the broadest

Harborne Hall Preparatory School for Boys, 1919–24

lines, having regard to the equipment with which every boy must necessarily be furnished when he leaves for his Public School. The formation of character is of paramount importance".

In the school magazine for 1919-20 the Head gave a description of the set-backs they suffered on trying to prepare the school for opening. The railway strike took place when a considerable amount of furniture and equipment was "on the line" and they suffered the "perennial servant problem".

Harborne Hall Preparatory School. An event on the terrace

The chapel was dedicated on 29th October 1919 by the School President, The Bishop of Birmingham, assisted by Revd. A Lloyd, Vicar of Harborne. The altar was decorated with lilies and the Bishop's address was reported in the *Birmingham Post*, 30th October 1919 — "the children who went from the school would know that if they were to do their duty in life they must try to live according to the will of Christ".

A popular feature in 1920 was the school tuck shop, each boy allowed specific rations and only the purest sweets and chocolates were purchased. The Headmaster realised the importance of good food for growing boys and provided the best quality available. For breakfast the boys had porridge, eggs and bacon (or fish), toast and marmalade, followed by milk and cake for elevenses. Lunch consisted of soup, joints and vegetables, sweets and cheese. Tea was bread and butter, jam and cake. Bread and milk or milk pudding was provided at bedtime and milk or cocoa was supplied after games. Hampers from home were therefore quite unnecessary.

All school sports were taught by expert men, including professionals who coached in cricket and football. There were three tennis courts in front of the Hall. The boys were coached on a nine hole golf course and shooting was taught in all weathers in open and covered ranges. Dancing classes were held in the winter on the fine floor in the hall.

The boys were drilled in deep breathing and put through essential exercises each morning. Gymnastics and boxing was also on the curriculum. Horse riding was available with weekly lessons and rides in the surrounding countryside were arranged for the advanced riders.

Harborne Hall Preparatory School. A school group

Gardening and nature study was much encouraged with each boy having his own garden which resulted in much rivalry in the production of flowers and vegetables. Botany was taught in the gardens so that a knowledge of natural history was acquired almost without effort.

The Headmaster's wife, Mrs Lawson, supervised the domestic arrangements and the care of the boys' health, assisted by a qualified Matron. On Sundays the boys attended church or school chapel and were encouraged to visit the Headmaster's study for a chat later in the day. In the afternoons they were able to enjoy country walks or the spacious grounds.

All these many activities in the school abruptly ceased in 1924 when the school suddenly closed. No explanation has been given for its failure except a suggestion that perhaps the boys were fed too well! The prospectus certainly indicates it was a very well equipped and enlightened educational establishment for five years.

The Sisters of La Retraite (1925-1988)

After numerous rumours of a nine-hole golf course development the Hall was bought again by a Roman Catholic community of Sisters of the Retreat of the Sacred Heart, just beating Anglican Deaconesses who were also interested in the property. The deal was completed in September 1925. The

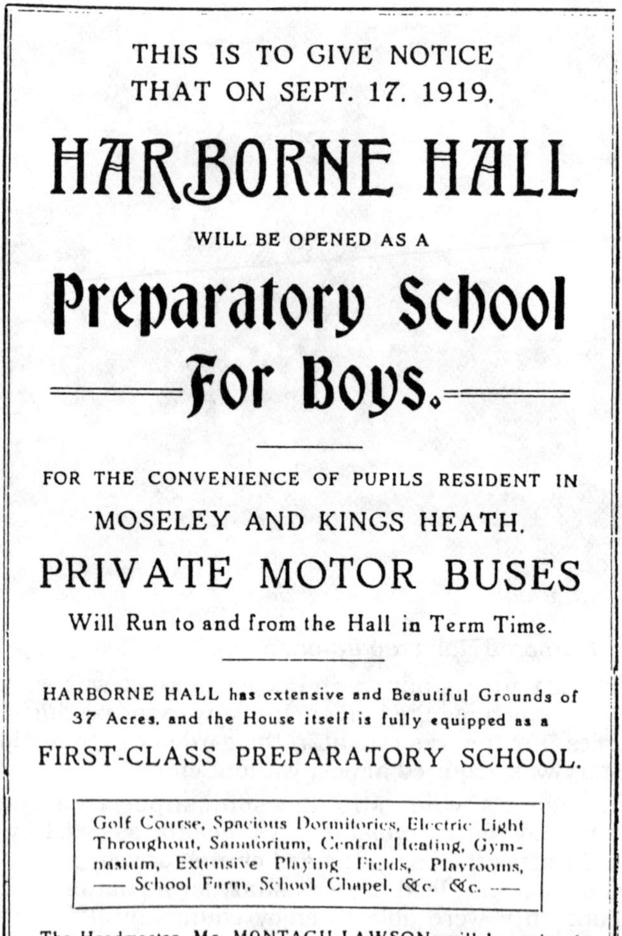

THIS IS TO GIVE NOTICE
THAT ON SEPT. 17. 1919.

HARBORNE HALL

WILL BE OPENED AS A

Preparatory School
For Boys.

FOR THE CONVENIENCE OF PUPILS RESIDENT IN

MOSELEY AND KINGS HEATH.

PRIVATE MOTOR BUSES

Will Run to and from the Hall in Term Time.

HARBORNE HALL has extensive and Beautiful Grounds of 37 Acres. and the House itself is fully equipped as a

FIRST-CLASS PREPARATORY SCHOOL.

Golf Course, Spacious Dormitories, Electric Light Throughout, Sanatorium, Central Heating, Gymnasium, Extensive Playing Fields, Playrooms, —— School Farm, School Chapel. &c. &c. ——

The Headmaster. Mr. MONTAGU LAWSON. will be assisted by a Full Staff of University Graduates.

For appointment to view the School. or for Prospectus. apply 125. ANDERTON PARK ROAD. MOSELEY.

Harborne Hall School advertisement

42

Hall was "in a perfect state of repair" and included 34 acres of land, being sold for £7,750.

Retreats dated back to Vannes in Brittany, France, in the seventeenth century. Seeing the success of the house of retreats for men in the same city, some ladies, led by Mlle. Catherine de Francheville, "joined together to form a community in which they would consecrate themselves to this work, to help people whom Providence would send, to benefit from the retreats".

The Convent — Harborne Hall, 1930s

Catherine de Francheville was from a well established family, having a deep faith beyond the usual commitment of a pious young woman, concerned for the poor. With her inherited fortune she started retreats for women in her own house in 1662. Her Rule of Life was "Let your only concern be to love and serve God, and the other person". The church authorities were suspicious of these women's meetings which were not held in religious houses so they were banned until a bishop authorised them in 1674. Catherine died in 1689, in the year her community was formed, called the Community of the Daughters of the Blessed Virgin. After the French Revolution all retreat houses were closed but in the nineteenth century they joined together to take the work forward, emphasising the educational aspect of the work. Now the successors to her movement are simply called "the Sisters of La Retraite" who are aware of the great needs of our age, a generation where unhappiness and lack of direction mark the lives of so many people.

In 1888 the order spread to Bruges when Mother St Benedict Labre started retreats at Prisonhof which became the Mother House as persecutions drove many nuns from France. She was instrumental in the

One of the Sisters of La Retraite at Harborne Hall

foundation of retreats in England. It was said of her "she had a heart of fire and lived for souls in entire self-forgetfulness, perpetually on the look-out for chances to do good". The Noviciate was housed there, where new entrants spent two years practising the religious life and receiving training which would enable them to instruct others and to give private retreats. A third year was spent there after vows were made, before they were sent out to undertake active work in a religious house. An important part of the work in Bruges was the instruction of converts — English priests from the large English colony in the town sent women to the nuns for instruction in the faith.

In the late nineteenth century a wave of anti-clericalism drove the Sisters from the retreat in Bruges. They visited four bishops in the north of England in 1909 seeking a place to settle but were unsuccessful until they visited the Midlands. The Ursulines in Great Malvern offered them a house in which they settled, holding their first retreat for twenty-five girls in July 1910. Most of the girls were poor and could not even afford to pay the 3/- asked for the retreat.

In 1912 a retreat house was opened in Birmingham in Wheeley's Road which was more suitable. They began children's retreats which were very popular but soon found the house too small and moved to a house on the Hagley Road in 1917. The house proving unsuitable they rented Penryn House in Somerset Road, Edgbaston, in 1919. Funds continued to be difficult — they charged retreatants between 5/6 and 10/- for a weekend, occasional gifts and donations were a godsend. In 1921 there was a great demand for places on retreats so they were considering purchasing Penryn, which belonged to a branch of the Chamberlain family, when someone told them Harborne Hall was up for sale. The last retreat at Penryn took place in October 1925, while the Sisters sorted rubbish and cleaned Harborne Hall.

On arriving at the Hall in 1925 the Sisters soon sold off some of the surrounding land to lessen their debts — a new Anglican school at St Peters was built. After adaptations to the building the convent opened with a students hostel and retreats began in 1926. In 1927 the Sisters wrote to many poor parishes inviting the priests to send people for retreats for half or quarter fees, or "any offering", such was their concern for the poor. In the 1930s there were many retreats — cash was short but retreatants plentiful. About forty-five could be taken at weekends — charges were low so that poor people could attend. In 1930 Archbishop Williams had given much encouragement to retreats, which "give you the necessary fuel, not only for your own spiritual life, but for the work among your fellow men". The Sisters also had an income from women boarders — students, professional women and old ladies.

Despite being in a country where Catholics were in a minority the retreats were successful, "education clearly marked by the old values of respect for the poor, of respect for individuals and of faith in small beginnings". Harborne became an important factor in the development of Catholic life in the Midlands. According to one of their publications, the work of the society of the Retreat included nursing, care of the aged, catechism instruction, language teaching, secretarial work, book keeping, domestic arts, gardening, and sacristy work. The aim of the society was twofold: personal sanctification and the sanctification of others. The Sisters of the Retreat "combined the roles of Martha and Mary, leading a life of prayer welling over into action, and a life of action founded on and penetrated by prayer."

In the 1930s many of the Sisters could not speak English which caused a few problems for Harborne tradesmen. Few of the Sister ventured outside, apart from the Mother Superior, and on those occasions umbrellas were always carried for protection. The Sisters looked after the beautiful grounds of the Hall but had maids in the house and a gardener to tend the vegetables in the kitchen garden. Angora rabbits were also kept and the fur was sold.

The Sisters always provided a bowl of soup and a hunk of bread for the daily visitors known as "the Gentlemen of the Road" — they had to stand and consume it in the passageway, recalls a tradesman. The Sisters also spent many hours throughout the year making children's toys in readiness for a party held at Christmas for Harborne children. This was quite an event for many years. On collecting their children at the end of the afternoon parents became accustomed to seeing the usually sedate and decorous Sisters skipping around, skirts hitched up, playing games with the children. Each child was given a home-made toy to take home at the end of the party.

At the outbreak of World War II some nuns from retreat houses at St Omer, France, and Bruges escaped from the German invasion. They fled to England by cargo boat, after being bombarded in Calais. British authorities were sympathetic — they were brought to Harborne Hall by the voluntary service of drivers who usually transported troops.

Further alterations to the Hall were made in 1958 including thirty rooms, all equipped with hot and cold running water, radiators and divan beds. There were retreats for schoolgirls and "days of recollection" for mothers and Catholic women's organisations. Countless men and women appreciated the time of peace and quiet at Harborne Hall retreats, devoting themselves to prayer and thought, away from the noise of the world and cares of everyday life.

In 1964 a fine new chapel was made possible by the sale of land, reducing the grounds to seven acres. By 1971 retreats were still in demand for what the Revd. Mother described as "spiritual regeneration — a renewal of contact with God". Some 1,400 people attended retreats in 1970, coming from a radius of 30-40 miles and over 500 attended study weekends.

By 1988 the Sisters had begun to diversify their work to meet the needs of the times, giving spiritual support in parishes, hospitals, schools and universities. The same year they graciously offered to rent the Hall to the Multi-faith Centre.

MOSAIC — the Multi-Faith Centre 1988 to the present day

MOSAIC, a Foundation for Education and Citizenship, is an innovative educational venture dealing with the two most powerful currents in world affairs at the end of this century, i.e. religion and ethnicity.

The logo of the Multi-Faith Centre. The symbols are, reading clockwise,: Jewish, Muslim, Hindu, Buddhist, Sikh, Christian.

It is a Registered Charity (No. 543736) with directors representing the Hindu, Muslim, Sikh, Buddhist, Jewish and Christian communities. The teaching team are also members of these six traditions.

The Centre was initiated in 1981 following a three year intensive research project in which 156 people from fourteen Birmingham communities participated. They included Anglican, Baptist, Buddhist, Chinese Evangelical, German Lutheran, Hindu, Jewish, Methodist, Muslim, Pentecostal, Quaker, Roman Catholic, Sikh and United Reformed traditions.

The project was successful in testing and developing an education methodology for inter-faith and inter-cultural dialogue, and designs and makes possible annual residential programmes for groups from Sweden, Denmark, Germany, Belgium and Holland.

The aim of the Centre is to provide 'Education by Encounter', with a permanent team of multi-cultural educators and resource personnel from their communities. The team designs and implements a variety of programmes to meet the specific needs of particular groups: teachers, social workers, health workers, prison officers/chaplains, church personnel and university groups. Over the years staff and clients have built up a relationship of understanding, learning and respect for others which helps to promote harmony in a multi-cultural society.

The history of Harborne Hall has the theme of religion running like a thread through the last two hundred years, from the foundation of the Harborne Sunday School in the eighteenth century to MOSAIC, the Multi-Faith Centre, today. The Hall has a rich legacy of local and national history, being part of the Manor of Harborne, and the development of industrial Birmingham. In the Hall's peaceful secluded grounds one can easily imagine some of the earlier occupants enjoying their rural retreat. It is hoped that future generations will have the opportunity of appreciating the unique heritage of Harborne Hall.

Bibliography

ABRAHAMS, R.C. *History of Harborne*, 1956
COUNSELL, M. *History of Harborne*, 1989
CROFTON, A.J. *Genealogical Account of the Nettlefold Family*, 1963
ELLETSON, D.H. *The Chamberlains*, 1966
GILL, C. *History of Birmingham, Vol 1*, 1952
HACKWOOD, F.W. *Some Records of Smethwick*, 1896
HARDWICK, W.E. *Articles on the History of Harborne* (in Harborne Library)
HART, C.J. *History of the 1st Volunteer Battalion of the Royal Warwickshire Regiment*, 1906
KENWARD, J. *Harborne And Its Surroundings*, 1885
McKENNA, J. *Watch And Clock Makers of Birmingham*, 1990
PRESTERNE, T. *Harborne Once Upon A Time*, 1913
SKIPP, V. *Making of Victorian Birmingham*, 1983
SOLLY, N. *Memoir of the Life of David Cox*, 1873
WILSON, W. *Life of George Dawson*, 1905
WRIGHT, D. *Account of Harborne*, 1981
Dictionary of Business Biography
Dictionary of National Biography
Victoria Country History Vol 7. Warwickshire
Edgbastonia, Vol XXIII, Apr 1903
Midlands Captains of Industry, 8 Apr 1908
Midlands Antiquary, Vol 1, 1890/91

Index

Anglesey, Marquess of 10
artists 17
Ashley House 16
Attwood, Thomas 16
Avery Historical Museum 38
Avery, W. & T. Ltd. 32, 37, 38
Avery, William 32

Belgian refugees 36
Bewdley 3
Birch, Charles 18
    George 4, 5
    Sir Thomas 4
    Thomas 4
Birmingham 11, 13, 18, 24, 34, 35, 44
    Academy of Arts 17
    Agricultural Society 33
    Archaeological Society 23
    Art Gallery 12, 14, 18, 24
    Canal Navigation Co. 33
    General Dispensary 12
    General Hospital 19, 25
    School of Art 24
Bishop's Croft 5, 27
Blakeley Hall 3, 4
brass foundry 6
British and Foreign Bible Society 6
Bruges 43, 44, 45
buses 39

Cambridge 33
Canada 26
Cannell, Mr 38
Central Insurance Co. 32
Chamberlain clock 24
Chamberlain, Agnes 26, 28, 30
    Basil 28
    Herbert 26, 28
    John Henry 19, 28
    Joseph 13, 22, 24, 26, 28, 29, 33, 34
    Mary 24, 29, 30
    Pearl 28
    Walter 26, 27, 28, 30, 31, 32, 33, 36
chapel 40, 46
Charles Churchill & Co. 32
Charles II 3
Church Lads' Brigade 25
Church of the Saviour 12, 13, 14
Cobham 32
convent 44

Cornwallis, Sir Charles 3
    Sir Thomas 3
Coventry 1, 7
Cox, David 15, 17, 18, 33
curates 7

Dawson, George 12, 13, 14, 26
Domesday Book 1
Dudley, Edmund 2
    Lord Edward 3
    Sir John 2

Ecclesiastical metalworkers 18
Edward III 1
Edward Street 12
Edward VI 2
Edward VI Free Grammar School 6, 7
Elizabeth Tudor 2

Fellowes Lane 5
Fire Brigade 23, 25
First Volunteer Battalion of Royal Warwickshire Regiment 19, 20
First Warwickshire Rifle Volunteers 20
FitzGerald, Henry 1
    Warin 1
Foley, Thomas 3
Francheville, Catherine de 43
Freeman, William 15

Gas supply 16
Gisborne, Charlotte 7
Glover, Henry 3
golf course 40
Gooseberry Grower's Society 19
Graham Street 12
Great Malvern 44
Green Road 25
Green, Elizabeth 6
    Thomas 4, 5
    Thomas jnr. 6
Greenfield House 17
Greenfield Road 15
Grey, Lady Jane 2, 3
Grove House 16, 19
Guardians of the Peace 1
Guest, Keen and Nettlefold (GKN) 32, 33

Halesowen Abbey 1, 2
Hamstead 4

Harborne 1, 2, 3, 4, 5, 7, 8, 9, 15,
  17, 19, 22, 23, 25, 31, 34, 35, 45
Harborne & Edgbaston Institute 23
Harborne Board School 31
    Express 19
    Hall, architects 26
        architecture 5, 27, 28
        building of 4, 5
        exotic art 28
        extensions 26, 27, 45,
        46
        painting vi, 15
        porch 28
        staircase 28
        windows 27, 28
    House 5, 6, 8
    Liberal Unionist Association 32
    Manor of 1, 2, 3, 4, 5, 6, 8, 10,
    16
    National Society School
        Scheme 19
    Room, The 19
    Sunday Schools 5
    Tenants Ltd 34
    Volunteer Fire Brigade 23, 25
    Young Men's Friendly Society
    25

Hart & Son 18, 20
Hart, Bertram 25
    Charles 18, 19, 25
    Charles Joseph 19, 20, 21, 22,
    23, 24
    Dr George 18, 25
    Son, Peard & Co. 18, 19, 24
Harts Green 6
Hearth Tax 3
Heath Road 25
Heaton, Mrs 37
Henry II 1
Henry III 1
Henry VI 1
Henry VIII 2
Henry, Prince of Wales 3
Highbury 26, 28
Hillyfields 30
Hinckley, Henry 4
Holt Hill 4
horse bus 16
hospital 36, 37, 38

Iron trade 3, 5, 16
iron work 18, 20, 24

James I 3
jewellery business 11
John, King 1

Joseph Lucas Ltd. 32
Justice of the Peace 5, 6, 7, 24, 34

Kenrick, Mary 30
Key Hill 16
Key Hill House 15
King's Arms 16
Kingdon-Simcox, Revd. Henry 10
Kings Norton 9, 26
La Retraite, Sisters of 42, 43, 44, 45,
    46
Labre, Mother St Benedict 43
Lappal Tunnel 5
Law, Revd. James Thomas 7
Lawson, Monatagu 39
Lawson, Mrs 41
Lay Subsidy Roll 1
Lea, Hannah Maria 6
Leamington Spa 24
Lichfield 1, 2, 7
Livery Street, Birmingham 6
Lloyds Bank 33
London & North Western Railway Co.
    33
Longdon, manor of 1, 2
Lord of the Manor 1, 2, 3, 4, 5, 6, 8,
    10, 16
Lowe, Mrs Conway 37

Manor of Harborne 1, 2, 3, 4, 5, 6, 8,
    10, 16
Martin and Chamberlain 26, 27
Mary, Queen 2, 3
metalwork business 16, 18, 19, 23
Metchley Abbey 18
Middlesex 2
Midland Liberal Unionist Association
    33
Midlands Arts Club 24
MOSAIC 46
Mount Zion Chapel 13
Multi-faith Centre 46

Nail making 5, 9, 16
Nettlefold & Chamberlain 26, 33
Nettlefold, Clara Grace 33
        Edward 33, 34, 35
        Edward John 33
        J.S. & Sons 33
        John Sutton 26, 33
        Joseph 33
        Joseph H. 33
        Katherine 33
        Mildred 33
Newfoundland Government 38
Nicholson-Kingdon, Hannah 9
Northumberland, Duke of 2
Norwich 15, 17

49

Old British School 31
Old Swinford Hospital 3
Overlordship of the Manor 1, 2

Paget, Sir William 2
Penryn House 44
Piner family 5
postal service 16
Pratt, Elizabeth 6
Preparatory School For Boys 39, 40,
    41, 42
prison 5
Prisonhof 43
Protestant Dissenting Charity School
    12

Railways 19, 33
Redvers, Margaret de 1
religious education 5, 9, 13, 14, 43,
    44, 45, 46
retreat houses 45
Retreat of the Sacred Heart 42, 43,
    44, 45, 46
retreats 43, 44, 45
Roberts, Mary Jane 5, 15, 16
        Revd. E 25
        William 11, 15, 16, 17, 18
Round House 5
route marching 21
Royal Warwickshire Regiment 19, 20,
    21, 22

Salvation Army 25
school 39, 40, 41, 42
school chapel 41
school farm 39
schools 3, 7, 12, 19, 31
screw industry 26, 33
Selly Oak 25
Serpentine Road 23
Simcox & Pemberton 6
Simcox family 5
Simcox, Edward George 6, 7
        Elizabeth 7
        George 5, 6, 7
        George Gisborne 7
        Thomas 10
        Thomas Green 6, 7, 8, 9, 16

Sisters of La Retraite 42, 43, 44, 45,
    46
Smethwick 1, 2, 3, 4, 8, 9, 26, 33
Soho Foundry 32
Soho Trust 32
St Martin's Church 18
St Peter's Church 1, 2, 6, 7, 18, 19,
    22, 28
Staffordshire 2, 3, 7, 34
Stourbridge 3

Tariff Reform 34
Thompson, Ernest 14
Tipton 1
Tithe Map 6

Unett, John 8
Unionism 33

V.A.D. (Voluntary Aid Detachment)
    28, 36
Victoria, Queen 25
Volunteer Decoration 20, 23

W. & T. Avery Ltd. 32, 37, 38
War Lane 5
Warwickshire 6
water 7, 16
weighing machines 32
William the Conqueror 1
Williams, Archbishop 45
Wilmot & Roberts 16
Wilmot, Edward Dinwoody 11, 12,
        14, 15, 16
        Felicia 15
        Florence Nightingale Freeman
        15
        Jane 15
        John 11, 16
        Miss 18
        Phoebe 15, 16
        Rose 15
        Sarah 11, 15
Winchester 10
Witley Court 3
Worcestershire 3
Worcestershire Yeomanry 28
World War I 20, 28, 36

Zoo 30